Upgraded! How ~~~~~~~~~ and Fly in Luxury ~~~~~ Points

R. M. Edwards

Foreword & Copyright

Don't miss a hot deal or opportunity to earn more Avios!

Don't miss out on 'flash deals' or special offers which give you the chance to scoop bonus Avios points. These deals are often super-lucrative, but are easy to miss. As a 'thank you' for buying this book, I've created an exclusive mailing list which will ensure you don't miss any of the best offers. I promise no spam: I'll use it only to keep you up to date with the hottest Avios developments.

Simply visit www.flyupgraded.com and sign up.

All text and imagery copyright the author, 2016, unless otherwise stated. All rights reserved.

Legally, I can't make any warranty about the content of this guide. Information is provided on an 'as-is' basis, and I disclaim all liability arising from the use of information herein. Nothing in this book should be seen as constituting financial advice.

This is an unofficial work with no connection to Avios or any of its associated companies.

Where Could You Escape To With Avios?

With a bit of skill and knowledge, you can use Avios points ('Air Miles') to explore the world in style and luxury. If you fancy a short break in Europe or a First Class flight to the USA, you can use Avios points to secure discount tickets or great value upgrades.

Over the last couple of years, I've learned all the tricks and secrets of Avios points. And, having done so, I've been able to enjoy some amazing adventures - for much less than others might have paid. I've been able to secure last minute flights to Europe at hundreds of pounds less than the going price; I've flown in international First and Business class; and I've taken more short breaks and weekends away than I've ever done before. **You could do the same.**

I don't fly at all as part of my job, and I'm certainly not one of the world's 1% who could otherwise afford to pay for a Business class ticket. Instead, I've learned the ways to save Avios points, and where to find the 'sweet spots' to redeem them for great-value flight tickets.

I'll describe some of my most recent adventures for you, to give you a taste of the power of the Avios scheme. **With the tips in this book, you'll be able to enjoy the same experiences.**

Fancy a European Break?

If you're keen to fly to Europe, Avios can help you secure great value tickets - even at the very last minute. For example, a couple of summers ago, my work project suddenly changed, and I had a the opportunity to join some of my friends for a few days in Spain. In the peak summer, though, even an EasyJet flight was priced at about £230 return. With Avios, I found - at the very last minute - a British Airways flight to a more convenient airport: with the total cash outlay of £35.

Or a Trip in First Class?

Here's another example of how Avios could benefit you. At the start of 2016, I splashed out and flew trans-Atlantic **First Class on British Airways**. Using the tips within this book, you could definitely do the same.

First Class is undoubtedly a very special experience. Before departure, in the exclusive Concorde Room lounge in Heathrow Terminal 5, you're offered all the complimentary drinks and cocktails you could wish for. The house champagne is Laurent-Perrier Grand Siècle, which costs *£100 a bottle* in the shops. There's an al-la-carte restaurant (everything complimentary, of course), and also a pre-departure spa.

On the eleven-hour flight to the Americas, I relaxed in a comfortable flat bed with fluffy duvet, and ate a three course meal accompanied by some really nice wines. After dinner, I enjoyed a glass of eye-wateringly expensive scotch, and changed into a luxurious set of (free!) pyjamas before snoozing for a good few hours before landing.

In fact, I'm still wearing those pyjamas now ;)

First Class is the most expensive and luxurious service offered by British Airways. The normal price of my trip, if I'd have paid for my ticket, would have been about £5,500. With Avios, I paid £550 for the airline taxes - and the rest in my frequent flyer points.

Or Would You 'Just' Settle for Business?!

Of course, if you'd 'just' like to travel in Business Class on British Airways, you can also harness the magic of Avios. In the past year, I've upgraded my seat to Business Class on a long haul flight, and it was a brilliant experience - not quite as overblown as First Class, but still great fun.

As well as a flat bed, you can enjoy a glass (or three!) of champagne, a great meal, and a peaceful environment to get some rest. You honestly feel fairly relaxed and awake when you reach your destination - rather than wiped out.

Business Class prices to America from London might be in the region of £2,000- £2,500 return. But, with Avios, you'll pay around £500 in taxes, and the rest of the cost in your frequent flyer points.

Does it all sound a bit too good to be true? Well, it's not! There's no real 'catch' with Avios, but you need to know what you're doing. A great many people waste their Avios points because they don't understand the ins and outs of the programme. It's more than possible for anyone to enjoy a flight in First, or Business, if you understand how the scheme works - and the 'sweet spots' to make the most of your points.

This book is written for anyone who might have begun collecting Avios (or 'Air Miles', as they used to be known) through their shopping at Tesco, or from flying a little bit with BA. It's written to give you a good understand of how the Avios programme works, and how you can exploit it to create trips of a lifetime.

This is your insider guide to Avios: an essential briefing on how to fly further, and in greater luxury, for less money. I hope you find the information useful, and you have some incredible trips as a result of it.

The Basics

What are Avios?

Avios points are a like a currency. As a rough guide - if you're cunning or careful - an Avios point might be worth 1p each. That's an easy number to get your head around, so it's the figure I use in most of this guide.

Avios are used as the 'currency' of different airlines and different loyalty programmes. Right now, British Airways and the Spanish airline, Iberia, give away Avios to their customers. (Later in 2016, Irish Aer Lingus will also start awarding Avios). Avios are also given away by some other travel and leisure companies. (Much more below).

Avios are big business: every five minutes, one million Avios are issued to collectors all around the world.

Because so many different companies use Avios as their loyalty currency, there are a number of different 'current accounts' which hold your Avios.

It doesn't matter which one you choose to 'save' in. Each Avios is worth exactly the same and you can easily transfer between the accounts if you need to. These different 'accounts' are just for convenience, as each 'account' is aimed at a different type of customer. You can open an account at each of the 'branches', if you wish - it's free.

- **Avios.com.** Avios.com is aimed at the casual leisure traveller. Avios.com allows you to earn Avios through schemes including a shopping portal, and to redeem on BA flights, and also flights with some other smaller airlines (such as Flybe). It also allows you to redeem on Eurostar; on hotels; and on wine and other gifts. Set up your account at www.avios.com.

- **British Airways Executive Club.** The BA Exec Club is aimed at people flying with British Airways and its partner airlines (the Oneworld alliance, which includes Iberia). If you take a flight with BA or its partners, you'll earn Avios points. (You'll also earn entirely separate 'tier points' - points which elevate your VIP status in the Exec Club. But that's outside the boundaries of this guide). Using the BA Exec Club, you can spend your Avios on flights with BA and its larger OneWorld airline partners.
Set up your account at www.britishairways.com/en-gb/executive-club.

- **Iberia Plus.** Iberia Plus is the frequent flyer scheme for this Spanish airline. It works a bit like the BA Exec Club. You can also save Avios here, but it's of limited interest to people in the UK, as it's predominately aimed at the Spanish.

- **Aer Club.** This is the frequent flyer scheme for Aer Lingus. It will open in Summer 2016.

Remember, you open multiple accounts and can transfer your Avios between them easily - usually instantly*. So it doesn't matter how many accounts you open.

*The small print is that Iberia behaves a bit differently, but this isn't an issue for now (there's a bit more at the end of this book).

> *Avios used to be called 'Air Miles'. When BA merged with the Spanish airline Iberia, they re-jigged the scheme and called the points Avios - a made up word from Avión, which is Spanish for aeroplane.*

How do I earn Avios?

This is the subject of the first section of this book. However, to give you an overview, you can earn Avios by:

- Taking flights with BA, Iberia, or other selected airlines;
- Converting your Tesco Clubcard points to Avios;

- Spending money on a credit card that gives you Avios;
- Staying at hotels that credit you with Avios;
- Hiring cars with firms that give you Avios;
- Shopping through an online portal.

What can I spend Avios on?

This is the subject of the last section of this book. However, the overview is:

- 'Free', upgraded, or money off flights (even in 'luxury' seats) on BA;
- 'Free' flights, even in luxury seats, on BA's Oneworld airline partners;
- 'Free' flights on smaller, more local airlines, including FlyBe and AirMalta
- Eurostar Tickets
- Wine, shopping, hotel rooms and car hire.

When I say 'free', I mean that you have no airfare to pay. You still have to pay the taxes and fees on the ticket, though.

What are the best things to spend Avios on?

Avios are particularly good value for buying:

- 'Reward Flight Saver' tickets on BA to Europe;
- Last minute tickets to any destination;
- Long haul flights on BA in luxury cabins;
- Upgrades from BA's Premium Economy seats to Business Class seats.

Much more is detailed later in the guide.

What are the worst things to spend Avios on?

It's generally a poor use of your Avios to spend them on:

- Wine or shopping from Avios.com;
- Certain European tickets which aren't a 'Reward Flight Saver'
- Long haul flights in BA's economy seats at off-peak times.

Much more on this is later in the guide.

Do Avios ever expire?

Only if you don't earn or spend at least one Avios, every three years. Which is very unlikely.

Can I share my Avios with my family?

You can set up 'family' accounts to share Avios. This means you can pool your earnings to reach your next goal. You're allowed to set these up from either Avios.com, or via the BA Executive Club.

You're technically only meant to have a family account with people who live at the same address as you.

Can I give away my Avios to someone else?

Yes. Via the British Airways Exec Club, you can transfer them to anyone in the UK, but there's a significant cost to transfer them. It's a bit complicated to give an estimate, as the charge works on a sliding scale, but it's about £5 to transfer each 1,000 Avios.

Can I buy Avios outright?

Yes, but it's almost always very bad value. Prices start from £35 per 1,000 Avios, although you'll get a 'sale' emails each year offering '30% off' or 'get 40% extra, free'. This is only worth buying if you desperately need Avios to reach a target.

> *If you're interested in buying, see* www.britishairways.com/travel/purchase-avios/public/en_gb

How do I move Avios between my different accounts?

If you have an Avios held in, for example, a BA Exec Club account and an Avios.com account, you can quickly and easily transfer your Avios between the two.

Within the online 'Account management' pages of the account you wish to transfer *from*, choose 'Combine My Avios' tab. From there, you can choose how many Avios to transfer, and where they should go. The transfer is instant, and there's no charge.

Earning Avios

How can I earn Avios from flying?

To earn Avios by flying, set up a BA Exec Club account. Then make sure you add your frequent flyer number whenever you fly on BA or its 'Oneworld' partners, which include American Airlines, Qantas, and Iberia.

You will collect Avios for every mile you fly, but the earning rate is much less generous than it once was.

> Just two years ago, a return economy flight to New York would have earned you enough Avios to claim a single ticket to Europe. No-more!

You earn greater amounts of Avios when you fly in luxury seats, or on more expensive, flexible tickets. Except in some very niche situations, it's not worth paying the extra for a flexible ticket simply to earn more Avios.

Other airlines, which are not allied to BA (not part of the 'Oneworld' group), are now beginning to give Avios to passengers. These airlines include FlyBe and Royal Air Maroc. (As they're not associated with BA, you need to add your Avios.com account number to these bookings in order to claim Avios).

How can I earn extra Avios through BA Holidays?

If you choose a package holiday with BA (technically through BA Holidays, a subsidiary of BA.com), there's often an Avios bonus associated with the booking. Sometimes this can run to a few thousand extra Avios.

It's obviously not worth booking an entire package holiday just to get a few thousand Avios, but there can be some advantages when you compare the price of a short break through BA.com to the cost of booking the hotel and flight separately.

Without getting too technical, BA often earmark their very cheapest airfares to bookings made via BA Holidays. The reason for this is that there's a very large mark-up on hotels, so they still make a decent profit on the transaction, whilst remaining competitive with the large package tour operators.

The upshot is that you can often find a flight and hotel priced more cheaply than if you bought separately. There are other advantages, too: the most significant being more flexible options for payment, as you often only need to pay a deposit upfront and the remainder closer to the date of travel.

> *As an example: one week in Gran Canaria for two adults flying economy, staying in a 3* self catering hotel - £317.50 each, plus 1,270 bonus Avios*
>
> *Booking the elements separately for the same holiday: £385 each, with no Avios*

See www.ba.com/holidays

How do I earn Avios from Tesco?

When you shop at Tesco and use a Clubcard, you'll earn Clubcard Points.

These can be exchanged for lots of different items via Tesco's online portal, and you can exchange Clubcard Points for Avios points.

The standard rate of exchange is that £2.50 in Clubcard points yields you 600 Avios.

There are two ways to exchange your Clubcard Points to Avios. You can amend your online account and set up 'Autoconvert', which means that every Clubcard point is automatically converted to Avios, and beamed across to your Avios account. The alternative is to save up your Clubcard vouchers and convert them manually on the Tesco Clubcard online portal.

Oddly, you'll often find that this second option is better value. Occasionally, perhaps once a quarter (no-where near as often as they once did) Tesco will offer a bonus when you convert your Avios - uplifting the conversion to 800 Avios per £2.50, for example. For this reason, it's worth sitting on your Clubcard points and waiting until you get an email telling you about a bonus offer.

Image by El Ronzo

Are there other ways to earn Clubcard points (and, then, Avios?!)

It can be quite easy to mount up a big total of Clubcard points. Tesco offer regular 'bonus' offers on certain products purchased in store or via Tesco Direct - 100 points for a pre-ordered book or CD, for example, or 1,000 points for buying a vacuum cleaner. Unfortunately, these deals come around a lot less often than they once did, but they're still worth it when they appear.

You might be surprised at the enthusiasm a lot of people feel for Avios - these deals often get snapped up as soon as they go online. Quite often, you'll find that people buy the products new and then re-sell them immediately on eBay or Gumtree, using the deal as a cheap way to turnover Avios. (The real enthusiasts will buy the item on a credit card which gives them Avios on purchases too - and also nudges them further to a 'spend target', for which they receive a special Avios voucher).

If you're interested, it's best to sign up for Tesco's promotional emails, and act quickly when a deal you're interested in comes to light.

Tesco also offer small monthly bonuses of Clubcard points if you complete a quick market research survey, rating your shopping experience online (see your receipt if you've recently shopped with them); or if you complete occasional, lengthy, market research surveys sent by their panel (full details can be found on their Clubcard portal).

One popular trick to generate quite a lot of Clubcard points is to get involved with Tesco's printer cartridge recycling scheme. Quite a lot of keen collectors have been known to liberate used printer cartridges from their workplace, or from friends and family, and to post them Freepost to Tesco's recycling partner.

The exact amount of Clubcard points you receive is dependent on the type of cartridge you send in, and it can be anywhere from 25-125 points per cartridge. As a few collectors got a little over-eager with this offer in the past, you're limited to the numbers of cartridges you can send in each year (presently 100 per household…!).

http://www.therecyclingfactory.com/tesco/

Tesco also offer longstanding bonus deals on buying giftcards - when you spend £50 on giftcards either instore or online, they'll award you 150 bonus points. As you can buy giftcards for big retailers (such as Topshop, Amazon, iTunes and Starbucks), it's quite a cunning way to earn extra Clubcard points if you were already planning to spend in these stores.

Tesco also provide financial services and, most notably, they'll award you 1 Clubcard point per £4 of your monthly mortgage payment with them. It goes without saying that you should absolutely never make a mortgage decision on based on getting some Clubcard points back each month, but don't miss out on this if you already borrow through them.

Earning Clubcard points with petrol

If you purchase fuel at Tesco, you can earn Clubcard points on the spend (presently one point per £2).

> Shell also offer you the opportunity to convert points in their loyalty scheme across to Avios.
>
> Because Shell petrol tends to be much more expensive than Tesco fuel, and because Shell's Avios exchange rate is pretty depressing (it works out as 10 Avios for 20 litres of standard fuel), the Shell partnership isn't something to get that excited about. It's better than nothing, of course.

Earning Clubcard Points via Topcashback

Until July 31st 2016, there's also a good trick to earn Clubcard points if you frequently shop online. You may have heard of 'cashback' sites: ones which give you a percentage of your purchase back if you buy through their site. The biggest players are Topcashback and Quidco.

> www.topcashback.com
> www.quidco.com

Most major retailers - from M&S to Debenhams - are listed on Topcashback, and you'll earn, on average, 2-3% of your purchase back in cash when you click through to their sites.

You can claim back your money in pure cash which can be transferred across to your bank account, or you can convert the cash to vouchers for use on Amazon.co.uk, for example. You actually get a little more value if you claim in vouchers rather than in hard cash.

Relevant to this guide, Topcashback offers you an option **to receive Tesco Clubcard points rather than cash.** You can convert up to £50 of your earned cashback into Clubcard points each year. You can then transfer these Clubcard points into Avios when the time is right.

To organise a Topcashback payout into Clubcard points, you need to go to the payout page on their website and check that you want to withdraw your money to Clubcard.

They have a slightly restrictive and confusing website. All your earnings are split into different credits, according to the merchant where you earned them. You need to select all the cash back credits which you'd like to be credited to Clubcard, up to a maximum of £50.

> If the grand total comes to more than £50 (let's say you have two credits in the bank, each for £30), there'll be a 'computer says no' moment and it won't let you convert the cash to Clubcard.
>
> The reason for this is because £60 is beyond the annual limit of £50, and it won't let you 'break' either amount.
>
> If this happens to you, simply donate the excess over £50 - so, in this example, the £10 - to one of the listed charities. You can then withdraw the rest to Clubcard.

You'll also notice that Topcashback offers you the option to directly claim Avios (ie, you convert your cash directly to Avios, rather than to Clubcard points and then need to convert again). Avoid this! The conversion rate directly from cash to Avios is much, much worse than using Tesco points as an intermediary. Unless you're absolutely swimming in cashback, avoid this tempting looking offer.

Earning quick Avios with Topcashback

You can make a lot of Avios quite quickly with Topcashback. Companies spend a lot of money acquiring new customers, and you'll find that there are generous amounts of money to be earned on your first online shop with Asda, for example, or if you move your mobile phone contract to another provider, or search for and purchase home insurance with another company.

You'll notice, too, that there is lots of cashback to be earned by signing up and placing a deposit with a gambling site. I would absolutely never suggest doing this if you've ever had problems with gambling in the past. However, if you've got iron-will and are confident that this isn't a pathway to financial disaster, you could consider signing up with one of these online gambling sites, making the pre-requisite deposit, and wagering enough to validate the claim.

It's worth reading the terms and conditions of these cashback offers very carefully - generally, any voucher code will invalidate your claim. Additionally, certain betting patterns don't as genuine wagers - putting money on both red and black in a game of roulette will, for example, invalidate the bet.

However, if you meet the offer conditions, you should be awarded the cashback - and, if you've got no further interest in using the site, you can withdraw your winnings and close your account (although I'd wait to do this until you've received your Topcashback to your Clubcard account).

Topcashback will stop paying out Clubcard points as of 31st July 2016, so you'll need to act quickly to claim these deals.

Are there other ways to earn big chunks of Avios?

There are other methods to earn big chunks of Avios quite quickly. One new sector - which is quite competitive at the present - is the online hotel booking portal. There are two large companies vying for your business - Kaligo and Rocketmiles. They award very large amounts of Avios in return for your hotel booking. Earning 2,000 - 3,000 Avios per night isn't uncommon, and these will be transferred quickly to your account after you stay.

Both sites offer a very wide range of hotels - probably as many as you'll find on hotels.com or with Expedia.

There's no definite answer if these hotel sites offer good, or poor, value for your money. You can occasionally stumble across hotels which are competitively priced and offer you thousands of extra Avios to boot; on other occasions, the hotels will be much more expensive than if booked through another online portal.

All you can do is compare the price offered on one of these aggregators with a competitor site (say Trivago, for example), and work out what's the best value.

> www.rocketmiles.com
> www.kaligo.com

Earning Avios through hotel loyalty programs

It's possible to earn Avios through non-competing travel loyalty schemes: for example, through the loyalty programmes for Hilton Hotels or IHG Hotels (the Holiday Inn/Intercontinental chain).

These chains will often let you either exchange the points you earn in their scheme for Avios points; or will let you earn Avios points directly when you stay with them, in lieu of their own points.

To be honest, it'd take an entire other book to thrash out which of these hotel loyalty schemes is the most worthwhile, and which offers the most generous earning opportunities if you're collecting Avios.

As a rough guide, it's worth considering converting your hotel loyalty scheme points into Avios if you don't stay in the chains particularly often, and if you won't earn enough to claim the free rooms or benefits that the hotels offer to frequent guests. However, check out the exchange rates and price up things carefully, as occasionally the transfer rates can be extremely poor.

Let's work things through. Imagine you're staying in the Hilton in Manchester - for ease, say it costs the equivalent of USD$150 a night. In their loyalty programme, you have two options: take your reward entirely in Hilton Points (2,250); or take part in Hilton Points, part in Avios (1,500 of theirs plus 150 Avios).

The cheapest redemption rooms at the Hilton chain start out at about 20,000 points a night. Which means that, if you choose the first option, you're more or less getting a tenth of a free night, for every night you stay. That's probably a bit more generous than the equivalent of £1.50 in Avios. However, it really depends on how often you're going to stay in a Hilton - if the Avios are more valuable than a bunch of points you might never use.

Earning Avios through other airline loyalty programmes

For obvious reasons, you can't easily exchange loyalty points obtained in competing airline loyalty programmes into Avios. For example, you'll struggle to convert Virgin Atlantic points into Avios: it's not like BA and Virgin are best friends.

(Okay, it's technically possible if you exchange these points to an intermediary hotel scheme, and then exchange on again to Avios: however, you'll lose out twice to poor exchange rates, so it's barely worth it).

Earning Avios through other travel services

As Avios is a travel brand, you'll often find Avios used as an incentive when you're booking car hire, or parking at an airport. These Avios bonuses are usually offered on both avios.com, and through the BA Executive Club portal.

The amounts of Avios offered tend not to be outstandingly generous - it's presently a minimum of 500 Avios for **hiring a car with Avis** and booking via the BA site.

However, there are some benefits to hiring this way: as a BA Exec Club member you're allowed a second driver without charge, and there are often bonus deals to increase the number of Avios earned per rental.

> www.avisba.com

If you're travelling to Heathrow, there are also bonus Avios offered on **tickets booked on the Heathrow Express**: 100 Avios for a single and 200 for a return. The Heathrow Express is costly, though, so I'm not sure if it's worth it.

If you're driving to Heathrow or Gatwick, there are also Avios incentives for booking parking with one of BA's partners.

> http://www.britishairways.com/en-gb/executive-club/collecting-avios/parking

Earning Avios through online surveys

It's really laborious, but it's possible to top up your balance of Avios by signing up to complete regular online surveys. There are two main providers: Rewards for Thoughts and eRewards.

> www.rewardsforthoughts.co.uk
> www.avios.com/gb/en_gb/collect/erewards/erewards

Rewards for Thoughts offers 600 Avios for your first competed survey, and 25-50 Avios for each survey you complete after that.

eRewards offers 750 on signup, and a variable amount after that.

Unless you have a lot of spare time to spend doing pretty boring consumer surveys, I don't think it's worth really engaging with either of these schemes. You need to complete a lot of surveys to earn small amounts of Avios.

I'd personally signup for both schemes, grab those initial free bonuses, and leave it at there.

Spending Avios

How Far Can I Fly With Avios?

Image by Basheer Tome

You can fly pretty much anywhere you'd like in the world with Avios. There are lots of different ways to use your points to claim a seat: here's the general overview.

1. You can redeem your Avios against the entire price of a ticket (you just pay taxes and fees). Particularly for flights in Europe, you might find that the best deals are with BA or Iberia. However, that doesn't restrict you into having to fly with them. You can choose a partner airline instead - any airline from Qantas to Qatar.

2. On BA, you can buy a cash ticket and then use Avios to upgrade to a more expensive seat. As an example, on a BA transatlantic flight, you could buy a Premium Economy ticket in cash, and then use Avios to upgrade to Business.

3. **On BA, you can a use Avios as a discount against the cash price of most tickets.**

Claiming Avios seats on British Airways or Iberia

British Airways guarantees that they'll make two Avios seats available in business and four available in economy, on every single flight. This counts for both short haul and long haul flights.

Iberia make similar guarantees.

These Avios seats open up at approximately 12 midnight (London time), 355 days before departure.

> **If you want an Avios seat on a popular long haul route (or a short haul route at a popular time like Christmas), you need to be up at 00.00, ready to book, 355 days before you want to fly. See later for more.**

The most popular routes, where you need to be super-organised, are listed below.

In addition to these six seats on every plane, British Airways often makes further seats randomly available, even up to twelve hours before departure.

There is no rhyme or reason when these additional seats will appear. It all depends on a number of computer algorithms which work out how many paid tickets BA has sold, how many they expect to sell, and how many seats are empty on the plane.

It is best to be realistic, however. On the most popular routes, where BA never struggles to fill their planes, these additional seats are seldom made available.

The computer programs which work out how many 'extra' seats they can give away for Avios are always churning away in the background. If there are extra Avios seats available on the flight, but they suddenly calculate that it's no longer worth giving away Avios seats (perhaps because they've just sold a number of expensive tickets), they'll whip the free Avios tickets off the market before anyone claims them.

Because of this, my advice to you is that if you see Avios tickets on a time and date that suits you, claim them immediately. You can always cancel them. In Avios, like in life, if you snooze, you lose.

Avios seats on other airlines

You can also redeem your Avios for seats on airlines which have no commercial relationship to BA. (You can only find these seats through avios.com). These often-forgotten partners are:

- Air Malta (flights from different UK airports to Malta)
- Air Auringy (flights to the Channel Islands)
- FlyBe (European holiday destinations)
- Monarch (European holiday destinations).

There is no hard and fast rule about how many Avios seats are available on each flight on these different airlines. You will need to search and see.

Searching and Finding the Avios Seat You Want

This is where things get a little complicated.

If you have a BA Exec Club Account, you can use their website to search and book Avios seats on the following airlines:

- BA & Iberia
- 'Oneworld' Partner Airlines (incl American Airlines & Qantas)

- 25 | flyupgraded.com -

- Aer Lingus
- Vueling (the low-cost airline based in Barcelona).

To book or search for availability, go to www.britishairways.com/en-gb/executive-club/spending-avios/reward-flights and click on 'Book a reward flight'.

If you have an Avios.com account, you can use their website to search and book Avios seats on the following airlines:

- BA & Iberia
- Aer Lingus
- Vueling (the low-cost airline based in Barcelona)
- Air Malta, Air Auringy, FlyBe, and Monarch.

However, it's even more complicated than this appears. You should know that Avios.com often lists a better selection of redemption seats on BA planes than British Airways do on their very own site!

> It's a totally stupid situation - without getting too involved, it's because Avios.com have access to the very cheapest 'fare bucket' of tickets.
>
> **Advanced Tip!** To add another level of complication, if you want to fly to or from Spain, it's worth also searching on Iberia Plus. Iberia have a better selection of their own cheap tickets.

Of course, you can have both an account at Avios.com and BA Exec Club, and can transfer Avios between them at any time at no cost. So there's no harm in searching widely.

As a rule of thumb, if you're travelling to Europe, you'll generally find that Avios.com offers you the best range of options.

How Much Will My Avios Booking Cost?

To claim your seat, you'll need to pay an amount of Avios, plus a sum in cash as 'taxes, fees, charges and surcharges'.

The Avios cost of a redemption flight depends on how far the flight is, and the date when it departs.

The easiest way of figuring this all out is to use the calculator on the BA website at www.britishairways.com/travel/avios-calculator/public/. However, if you want to work it out for yourself, you should know that BA have divided the world into nine zones. From London, zone nine is for ultra-long haul (to Sydney), and zone one is for very short flights (to Manchester). (A full chart is just below).

Generally, European flights fall in zones one to three. Flights to North America are zones five to six.

In addition to distance, BA have a calendar where every day of the year is broken into 'peak' and 'off peak' days. Obviously, the Avios amounts required for a redemption seat are lower on 'off peak' days.

> Inevitably, BA fiddle with this calendar all the time, so it's best to look at the latest version on their website. Essentially, peak dates coincide with school holidays.
>
> See http://www.britishairways.com/en-gb/executive-club/spending-avios/reward-flight-offers and click on 'Peak and Off Peak Calendar'

There's also a cash cost to these Avios redemption tickets. BA and Avios.com describe the price as the 'taxes, fees, charges and surcharges' which you'd pay on a normal ticket.

To put it bluntly, the 'fees and taxes' added are unfairly high and don't represent the true costs involved.

The exact taxes levied will vary depending on destination airport (due to airport taxes), travel class (as Business tickets attract higher taxes than Economy tickets), distance flown (due to 'fuel surcharge') and even passenger age! This cash component does not vary according to the 'off peak' or 'peak' days, however.

There's no exact table spelling these costs out. You need to begin a reward booking to see how much they want to charge you, or you can use the calculator at www.britishairways.com/travel/avios-calculator/public/.

However, as a rule of thumb, you could expect these charges to come to about £30 for a return Avios ticket to Europe in Economy, and £300 return to East Coast USA. (A Business return ticket might run to about £50 of taxes in Europe, and £500 to the US).

Single Reward Seat Cost in Avios, by Zone

	Economy		Premium Economy	
	Peak	Off-Peak	Peak	Off-Peak
Zone 1	4,500	4,000	6,750	5,750
Zone 2	7,500	6,500	11,250	9,500
Zone 3	10,000	8,500	15,000	12,750
Zone 4	12,500	10,000	25,000	20,000
Zone 5	20,000	13,000	40,000	26,000
Zone 6	25,000	16,250	50,000	32,500
Zone 7	30,000	19,500	60,000	39,000
Zone 8	35,000	22,750	70,000	45,500
Zone 9	50,000	32,500	100,000	65,000

Single Reward Seat Cost in Avios, by Zone (continued)

	Business Class		First Class	
	Peak	Off-Peak	Peak	Off-Peak
Zone 1	9,000	7,750	18,000	15,500
Zone 2	15,000	12,750	30,000	25,500
Zone 3	20,000	17,000	40,000	34,000
Zone 4	37,500	31,250	50,000	42,500
Zone 5	60,000	50,000	80,000	68,000
Zone 6	75,000	62,500	100,000	85,000
Zone 7	90,000	75,000	120,000	102,000
Zone 8	105,000	87,500	140,000	119,000
Zone 9	150,000	125,000	200,000	170,000

Evidently, the cash price of a return Business ticket could comfortably be between £2,000 and £3,500 - and so, even with the £500 of tax to pay, you're making a fantastic saving - it works out to about 1.5p of value per Avios spent.

However, a cash economy ticket to New York can be as little as £490 - only a £190 more than this 'free' ticket. So you're getting very poor value for those Avios - about 0.4p of value per Avios.

As a result of these expensive taxes and charges, it can mean that long haul Avios redemptions in Economy class can work out to be poor value.

The exception to this rule is during busy times of the year, when the cash prices are high anyway (around Christmas or Thanksgiving, for example).

At that time of year, you'd probably pay more than £1,200 for a cash ticket to New York. So, even if you have to pay about £300 in taxes and fees, it works out as a much better deal per Avios spent.

Avios and Short Haul (European) travel

It's worth saying that Avios are often excellent value when it comes to travelling in Europe.

There's often reasonable availability of free seats, and, if you're flying on BA or Iberia, **there's a special scheme called 'Reward Flight Saver'** which caps the amount of taxes, fees and charges you must pay on an Avios redemption ticket.

> In addition, if you don't have quite enough Avios to claim the ticket, BA will also allow you to 'part pay' for the shortfall in cash.

When you search for a ticket on Avios.com or via the BA Exec Club, providing you've earned at least one Avios in the last year, you'll be offered available **Reward Flight Saver tickets**. These are usually marked with a star, or highlighted.

Reward Flight Saver caps the charges on economy tickets to £17.50 each way (and so £35 return) or business tickets to £25 each way. You can mix classes (one leg economy, one leg business).

The cost in Avios depends how far you wish to fly in Europe (see the table above). The amount of Avios required will change depending on if you're flying on a peak or off-peak date (but there's no change to the cash component).

If you don't have enough Avios to buy the ticket, you will be given an option to purchase more. The cost is variable, and you'll be quoted on the booking page.

Some examples of total Avios Reward Flight Saver costs (return, off-peak)

- London to Paris - 8,000 Avios, plus £35
- London to Rome - 15,000 Avios, plus £35
- London to Athens - 20,000 Avios, plus £35

All these examples offer reasonable value for your Avios. If you compare the prices above to the cheapest possible fares with BA (which may not even be available on the day you travel), you'll get the value of about 0.7p - 1p per Avios point.

You'll notice that all these prices are for flights which start at London. So what happens if you don't live in London, then? Well, the bad news is that until quite recently, BA bundled in a domestic connection for free on these European Reward Flight Savers. So the price for Manchester via London to Athens (20,000 Avios plus £35) was the same as a direct London to Athens ticket.

Unfortunately, BA have axed this offer - making it a much less attractive deal for anyone outside London. You now need to either buy the Manchester to London leg separately, or shell out a full 8,000 Avios return for the shuttle between London and Manchester, in addition to the Athens ticket.

> *The one snippet of good news is that domestic connections are still 'free' with long haul Avios tickets.*

Cancelling Avios Bookings

There's something really useful about Avios tickets which people often overlook.

Avios Zones by Destination (from London) (Most popular routes listed)

The Avios Zones (from London)	Destinations (from London)
Avios Zone 1	Aberdeen, Amsterdam, Basle, Berlin, Bordeaux, Brussels, Copenhagen, Düsseldorf, Edinburgh, Frankfurt, Geneva, Genoa, Glasgow, Hamburg, Innsbruck, Jersey, Lyon, Manchester, Marseilles, Milan, Munich, Newcastle, Nice, Paris, Prague, Salzburg, Stuttgart, Toulouse, Turin and Zurich
Avios Zone 2	Algiers, Barcelona, Bari, Belgrade, Bologna, Budapest, Cagliari, Dubrovnik, Faro, Gibraltar, Helsinki, Ibiza, Lisbon, Madrid, Malaga, Naples, Oslo, Pisa, Rome, Stockholm, Tunis, Venice, Verona, Vienna and Warsaw
Avios Zone 3	Athens, Bucharest, Catania, Istanbul, Izmir, Kiev, Larnaca, Marrakech, Moscow, Paphos, Pristina, Sofia, St Petersburg, Thessaloniki and Tirana
Avios Zone 4	Cairo, Kuwait and Tel Aviv
Avios Zone 5	Abu Dhabi, Bahrain, Baltimore, Bermuda, Boston, Chicago, Doha, Dubai, Montreal, Muscat, New York, Philadelphia, Toronto and Washington
Avios Zone 6	Antigua, Atlanta, Barbados, Beijing, Bangalore, Calgary, Cape Town, Chennai, Dallas, Dar Es Salaam, Delhi, Denver, Entebbe, Grand Cayman, Grenada, Houston, Hyderabad, Johannesburg, Kingston, Las Vegas, Los Angeles, Lusaka, Mexico City, Miami, Montego Bay, Mumbai, Nairobi, Nassau, Orlando, Phoenix, Providenciales, Punta Cana, San Diego, San Francisco and Seattle
Avios Zone 7	Bangkok, Hong Kong, Mauritius, Rio De Janeiro, Sao Paulo, Shanghai and Tokyo
Avios Zone 8	Buenos Aires and Singapore
Avios Zone 9	Sydney

You can change, amend or cancel any Avios seat for a flat fee of £35. You'll be refunded the Avios you spent, plus the taxes and charges. (An additional £15 is charged if you contact the call-centre, rather than complete the refund online).

This means that Avios redemption tickets work a bit like fully-flexible, fully-refundable tickets, which are often hundreds of pounds more expensive than the usual non-flexible tickets you'd buy.

This gives you the luxury of being able to change your plans.

Avios and BA's 'Oneworld' Partners

As previously mentioned, you can redeem Avios for seats on British Airways' 'Oneworld' partner airlines. These include American Airlines, Qantas, Qatar, Finnair, and many others. You can only book these tickets via the BA Exec Club.

There can be big advantages to booking with one of these partners. BA is very London centric - whereas the other airlines have much better options if you'd like to fly from Manchester, Birmingham, or Edinburgh.

As before, there's an Avios cost plus a cash component in 'taxes'. When calculating the Avios, the standard zones apply - meaning the amount of Avios required is based on distance flown. However, the 'off peak' and 'peak' dates aren't a consideration - everything is treated although it's a 'peak' date.

When booking these tickets, the taxes and fees are a contentious issue. Quite simply, if you start you flight in the UK, BA will whack on a huge levy which includes 'fuel surcharges'. These will be in line with a normal BA redemption, as detailed above.

> It's worth pointing out that the airline you're about to fly with will see **none** of this cash - BA pockets it as profit. It's a bit of a scandal.

If, however, you book a Oneworld partner flight which begins and ends outside the UK, BA cannot charge you such exorbitant taxes. As an example, a Business class flight from Helsinki to Japan - rather than London to Japan - will cost you about £150 in taxes and fees, as opposed to close to £600. The Avios cost will be no different.

> *A BA Amex companion voucher cannot be used on an airline other than BA.*

How Do Seat Upgrades Work?

If you see an available Avios seat on British Airways, you can either claim it outright (as I described above), or you can upgrade to it.

There isn't a separate 'pool' of availability for seat upgrade opportunities. This means that the same seats offered as 'free' Avios seats are also seats which you can upgrade to. These upgrade opportunities are only offered on BA flights.

Using Avios held within a BA Executive Account, you can upgrade a paid-for ticket by one rung (or by 'travel class', in BA speak). It's often a savvy move.

> **In European short haul,** most BA planes are two class: Economy and Business. So you can upgrade an Economy ticket to Business using Avios.

> **On long haul flights,** the majority of BA planes have four classes: Economy, Premium Economy, Business and First. So you can use this trick to upgrade one class: from Premium Economy to Business, for example. Or from Business to First.

To upgrade using Avios, you'll need to have paid for the normal ticket in cash. Avios reward seat(s) need to be available in the cabin you want to upgrade into.

You can't do a 'leapfrog' double upgrade: paying once to upgrade to Premium Economy, and upgrading again for Business class.

Most cash tickets purchased through BA can be upgraded.

The exception to this rule is the cheapest Economy cash tickets, or heavily discounted sale tickets. These cannot be upgraded.

> *In technical terms, these are the tickets in fare 'buckets' Q, O and G and will often have been sold as 'Economy lowest'.*

To book or search for availability of upgrades, go to www.britishairways.com/en-gb/executive-club/spending-avios/reward-flights - the same page you'd visit to book a reward flight. Click 'book'.

From here, simply search for the times and dates for the flight you wish to upgrade. If a seat shows as being open for redemption, it's also open for upgrade. To make the upgrade, you can either call BA or log in, choose 'manage by booking', and then click 'upgrade using Avios'.

These upgrades are only administrated through BA Executive Club Accounts - they're not offered via Avios.com.

Some Limitations of Upgrades

If you're flying on a long haul BA plane which offers Premium Economy, it can often be tricky to upgrade your Economy ticket to a Premium Economy seat. This is for a number of reasons.

Many long haul Economy tickets sold in the UK fall into BA's 'cheapest' fare bracket, and so cannot be upgraded. But even if your ticket is upgradeable in theory, you will often struggle to find any seats available in Premium Economy. This is simply because BA only has a small handful of Premium Economy seats on each plane, and they also they make no guarantees about any PE seats being available at all for Avios customers.

Conversely, if you've bought a Premium Economy ticket, it's quite possible to upgrade to Business Class. Virtually all PE tickets are sold in the higher, upgradeable fare brackets, and there's many more Business class seats on each plane - and so more opportunity for upgrade.

> *If you've bought a ticket through BA that includes travel on American Airlines or Iberia, you can also upgrade these tickets using Avios. It's a little trickier and more restrictive, however, and the full terms are on BA's website.*

Why upgrading with Avios can be great value

Upgrading your seat with Avios can often be great value.

You can upgrade at any point: from the moment you purchase the ticket to just a few hours before flying. So it's very flexible. (You can't upgrade at the airport).

Evidently, you pay less Avios to upgrade than to book an Avios seat outright.

However - and this is a great benefit - you'll still earn Avios and also the 'Tier Points' for VIP British Airways status for the flight. These are calculated according to the original ticket you purchased.

Another great benefit is flexibility. BA only really begin to get an accurate idea of how busy their long haul planes will be between 36 and 12 hours before departure. At that time, they might start making more Avios seats available as they know the plane won't be full. You can then jump on the opportunity and upgrade a previously purchased seat to a more luxurious one.

As an example, it's quite common that Business seats become available in the final 24-8 hours before departure, and with a Premium Economy ticket, you can quickly upgrade and nab these. I've done this many times before.

The Ins and Outs Of Upgrades

The cost of upgrading with Avios is a little complicated.

Look at the table earlier in the book. You can see, at present, that to fly to New York in Premium Economy it costs 40,000 Avios one way (peak), and 26,000 Avios off-peak.

The cost of a Business Ticket is 60,000 Avios one way (peak), and 50,000 Avios off-peak.

If you buy a Premium Economy ticket in cash and wish to upgrade, the cost in Avios is the difference between the Avios total for the Business ticket and the PE ticket.

> So, **on a peak day**, that's 60,000 - 40,000 = 20,000 Avios one way. **On an off-peak day**, that's 50,000 - 26,000 = 24,000 Avios one way.

This is a very odd outcome - a glitch in BA's planning (it's not my error!). It's cheaper to upgrade on a peak day than it is to upgrade on an off-peak day.

There's another cunning trick to these upgrades. **You will still receive the Avios owed for buying a cash Premium Economy ticket.** In the example for NYC above, this is a minimum of 3,400 Avios one way. So you spend something, but you also get a little back.

The Cash Cost

There may be a small cash cost associated with upgrading your seat. This is the difference in tax (as there's higher rates in duty for Business class tickets than Economy class). It's difficult to estimate but this can be in the region of £50 long-haul, depending on route.

Booking With Cash & Instantly Upgrading With Avios

As well as upgrading previously purchased BA tickets, you can buy a ticket and instantly upgrade it with Avios (providing, of course, the upgrade space is available). Log in to your account and choose 'Buy with Cash and Upgrade with Avios'.

Using Avios instead of cash

BA also have new scheme to use Avios in lieu of cash, when you book a ticket on their website.

This scheme allows you to reduce the price of most BA cash tickets.

For example, if you're looking to buy a ticket to Spain that costs, say, £210 return, they will offer you the option to slice varying amounts off the cost:

- £75 off for 11,250 Avios;
- £50 off for 7,500 Avios
- £30 off for 4,500 Avios
- £10 off for 1,500 Avios

The discounts go up to £150 for long haul bookings.

The plus side of this new scheme is that it allows you to use your Avios - even small amounts - for a hard cash saving.

The bad news is that you're not getting a particularly good exchange rate for your Avios. With the rates above, you're effectively getting 0.66p per Avios.

It's much better value to book a reward ticket, if you're able. You should get better value per Avios, and there's the added benefit that the reward tickets are flexible and fully cancellable.

Problems finding Avios seats?

A lot of people get frustrated with the Avios scheme as they struggle to find the free seats they want.

Quite simply, Avios seats are in high demand, and it's not in BA's interest to give away things which people would happily pay full price for.

If you're very organised, or have dates more than a year out (for example, for a wedding in Australia), you could well be lucky. Because BA now guarantee a number of redemption seats in Economy and Business on each flight, you just need to be up early to grab them (see below).

However, **on these high demand routes,** it's rare that any more seats than the bare minimum will ever be released. As a result, these are **the routes where it's always very tricky to find Avios availability:**

- Australia (Sydney)
- Cape Town
- Singapore
- San Francisco/LA
- Most Caribbean destinations

Conversely, on these routes below, BA almost always has a bit of spare capacity. As a result, **you shouldn't ever struggle too much in finding an Avios seat**, whether you're booking three months, three weeks or even three days ahead:

- New York
- Boston
- Washington
- Seoul (South Korea)
- Mexico City

Expert Tip: Grabbing Competitive Avios seats

If you're planning to nab an Avios seat that's in high demand, it's important to note that these seats begin being 'loaded' on the system from 00.00 British Time, 355 days before departure. You need to be logged on at that time, and ready to act quickly to nab your seat.

If nothing appears at the stroke of 00.00, don't necessarily fret. It may not mean someone's beaten you to it - it's perhaps because it sometimes takes BA a little while to 'load' the seats onto their system. Keep retrying up to 01.00, just in case.

Of course, you'll only be able to grab the outbound seats for your trip at this time. You're going to need to repeat this process in a week/two weeks (or however long your trip will be!) in order to get the return ticket!

In these competitive cases, it's never worth waiting for the return availability to come online before booking the outbound. You'll certainly lose your first leg if you hang about like that.

Still Not Finding the Seats You Want? Try, Try and Try Again

If you don't secure your Avios ticket to Australia one year-in-advance, you've probably had it. However, for the majority of other routes at most other times (Christmas and popular holidays notwithstanding), you may find that BA release further seats, at entirely unexpected times, with no logic as to what comes available and when.

As previously mentioned, on long haul flights, a good amount of re-jigging goes on between 36 and 8 hours before departure, and seats may suddenly open up. But, before then, you may find that small batches of seats are suddenly released on odd days - it all depends on what the computer program says each day.

If you're desperate for a certain route at a certain time, it's worth searching the BA website most mornings to see if any availability ever opens up (and if it does, book it immediately). If you've been searching for a couple of weeks and nothing ever seems to be offered, it's probably bad news… but don't entirely give up just yet….

If All Else Fails….

If you're really struggling to find Avios seats to the destination you want, it can sometimes be worth thinking a little creatively. Often, it's possible to find the right trip at the right dates: it might just need a little bit of routing.

Here are some ideas….

- **Could you turn a single-stop holiday into a fly-drive?** For example, it may make more sense to fly into LA and out of San Francisco (or vice versa) rather than in and out of one city. In Europe, how about Nice to Bordeaux? Or Seville to Malaga?

- **Could you fly to an adjacent airport and then travel to your final destination?** As an example, suppose you wanted to go to Dubai - a very popular destination for people hunting for Avios seats. Could you instead try Abu Dhabi or Ras Al-Khamah? Both are about ninety minutes drive from Dubai. Alternatively, suppose you wanted to fly to California - again, a very popular destination. BA also flies to smaller Californian airports including San Jose - which is effectively downtown San Francisco.

- **Could you fly to a hub airport, and then book a separate connecting ticket?** It's very easy to find Avios seats to New York - could you then book an American Airlines ticket to say, Chicago, from there? (See the last section of this book if you wanted to find that ticket on the cheap!).

If only the outbound or only the inbound flight is available, and the flight is inside Europe, **could you book a single ticket with another airline?** (I know, I know: it does feel a bit like giving up…!). However, with European airfares, there should be no penalty for booking one leg with Avios, and the other leg with Easyjet. (Sadly, it's not often possible to book long haul single tickets, often for visa/immigration reasons).

> *This is the subject of a whole other book, but, for destinations to the USA, you could join Virgin Atlantic's frequent flyer scheme. Some flyers are able to book one leg with BA and, if the other leg isn't available on BA, search within the Virgin loyalty programme. Unfortunately, I haven't the time or expertise to go into the Virgin programme in great length: if you're willing to research it yourself, you might find some options open up for you.*

Collecting Avios and Valuable Vouchers Through Credit Cards

If you want to earn a lot of Avios quickly, signing up for a credit card is a neat way of doing this. Many credit cards also give you Avios points for your regular day to day spending, making it relatively easy to rack up a flight or upgrade.

In addition, some of these credit cards give very useful vouchers upon reaching certain spend targets. These bonuses can help you make more of your Avios.

If you've had a history of credit card debt, or you've got outstanding loans, I really, really do not want to encourage you to take on an extra liability.

However, if you have a good credit rating and will be able to repay your balance in full each month, you could consider opening up one of these credit card accounts. It's important to note that all these credit cards have high APR rates, meaning that they would often be poor choices for borrowing money - if you open up any one of these, make sure you repay your balance on them.

It's also worth noting that there will be major changes to these Avios credit cards in the next couple of years. New legislation means that it's much trickier for the credit card companies to offer such generous deals. Of course, who knows what will change - but if the below offers look good to you, it might be wise to jump on board sooner than later.

British Airways American Express Card & BA Premium Plus American Express

If you're a big spender, or relatively serious about collecting Avios, this card could well be worth consideration.

BA offers two credit cards through American Express. The 'standard' card has no annual fee. The 'premium' card has an expensive annual fee of £195.

On the standard card, you earn 1 Avios for every £1 you spend. On the Premium Plus card, you get a higher 1.5 Avios per £1.

The 'usual' sign up bonus is 3,000 Avios for opening the standard card (when you spend at least £500 in three months). For the Premium card, you get 18,000 Avios if you spend £3,000 in three months.

There are frequent promotions and offer periods where the sign up bonuses are increased (usually to 6,000 Avios and 22,000 Avios respectively).

The really big bonus of these cards is the companion voucher. If you spend £20,000 in one year on the standard card, or £10,000 in a year on the Premium card, you'll receive a very valuable 'two for one' voucher. More about this voucher is written later in this book, but it allows you and a partner to travel together on a return Avios flight, paying only the Avios for one ticket.

£10,000 is a lot to spend on a credit card in a year; £20,000 is a very large amount. However, if you have a good chance of getting to £10,000 but no chance of spending £20,000, I'd strongly consider paying £195 for the Premium card. (If you have no chance of meeting either threshold, the free card is fine).

This is because the two for one voucher opens up some huge opportunities, and you'll also get 50% more Avios for your £195 investment (that is, an extra 5,000 Avios if you make the £10k spend threshold).

Lloyds Bank Avios Rewards Duo Pack

Lloyds has a complicated package of Avios credit cards. There is the 'Avios Rewards' Credit Card Account, and the 'Premier Avios Rewards' Account. **I also own these cards, and they've worked well for me.**

Each of these Lloyds accounts comes with two cards - an American Express and a Mastercard. Despite this, you only have one account - one credit limit, one monthly statement. You can use the cards interchangeably. The only difference is that the American Express Card earns many more Avios than the Mastercard.

With the standard account, you earn 1.25 Avios per £1 spent on the Amex, and 1.25 Avios per £5 spent on the Mastercard.

With the premium account, you earn 1.5 Avios per £1 on Amex, and 1.5 per £5 on Mastercard.

On both cards, there're no charges or foreign exchange fees when you use your card abroad. This is a really good bonus - these fees can sometimes be 3-4% of anything you buy. If you go on holiday or abroad for work and use a credit card, this can add up to an excellent deal.

If you reach certain spend targets, the cards also offer a good bonus. If you get to £7,000 spend on the standard card (£5,000 on the premium) during one calendar year, you get a free 'upgrade for two' voucher.

This voucher allows you a 'free' Avios upgrade for one person for a return flight, or two people flying a single leg.

If you have the premium card and reach £12,000 of spend, you get a further bonus. This is a 'companion voucher'. If you book an economy Avios seat, a friend can come along for free with you - they just need to pay the taxes and charges.

The standard card has a cost of £24 a year. Because you can earn Avios on it, and because you have no foreign exchange fees, this is often £24 well spent.

The premium card costs £140 a year. This is ridiculously expensive! I cannot see any real benefit to having this premium card - it really only earns a measly 0.25 extra Avios per £1, and the extra companion voucher isn't particularly generous.

TSB Avios Credit Card Duo Pack

TSB also offer a 'duo pack' of a MasterCard and an American Express card, linked to one credit card account.

TSB's selection isn't dissimilar to the Lloyd's scheme, although I'm not quite sure if it offers the same value. There's a 'standard' account, which is free to open, and offers 1 Avios per £1 spent on the Amex and 1 Avios per £5 spent on the MasterCard.

The 'Premier' account costs £50 a year, and it offers 1.25 Avios per £1 on Amex, and 1.25 Avios per £5 on the Mastercard. It also has a 'companion voucher' benefit. If you spend £15,000 a year, you get a free ticket for a friend when you redeem Avios for an economy seat.

Both accounts also offer double Avios for overseas spend (although you have to pay the usual foreign exchange fees, which makes this very unattractive). There's also an interesting benefit up to December 2016 - you can add the cards to Apple Pay, and you get 5% cash back on your first £100 of Apple Pay transactions each month.

I value the overseas spending benefits on the Lloyds card, plus I think the free voucher offered is much more generous on that card. But you might feel differently!

American Express Gold Card

This card is the 'odd one out' in two ways. The first: it doesn't directly earn Avios. Instead, it earns American Express Reward Points. You get 1 point per £1 on most spend, and £2 when spent on air travel. You can exchange these points for a variety of things: including Avios. The present exchange rate is 1:1 although, a few years ago, it used to be possible to get a better exchange rate during certain offer periods. I'm not sure we'll see this deal again.

The Gold Card isn't a credit card: this is the second odd thing! Instead it acts as a charge card. Essentially, with a charge card, you need to repay the balance in full every month. It doesn't offer you the opportunity for credit.

Amex Gold has an annual fee: £140 a year. However, it will be waived in your first year. For your money, you also get membership to 'Lounge Club' - a programme where you can get paid-for lounge access at many airports. Each year, Amex will give you two free visits.

You'll also be given insurance against travel delays, and some hotel and car hire discounts.

You get a very generous welcome bonus for signing up to this card: 20,000 points if you spend £2,000 in three months. Sometimes, during promotional periods, this bonus is even higher.

Tesco Bank Credit Cards

It's worth mentioning Tesco's selection of credit cards, too. They offer a number of different cards, each designed for slightly different purposes - cards for balance transfer, for examples, or cards with an extended interest free period if you've got a big purchase coming up.

They also offer Tesco Clubcard points on the transactions made on these cards, although the points involved are hardly generous. The present earning rate is one Clubcard point per £8 spend outside Tesco, and one Clubcard point per £4 spent in Tesco (in addition to your regular earnings from shopping). There is no annual fee on any of their cards, but there's no sign-up bonus, either.

Where the Tesco cards might benefit you is that they've slightly more competitive APRs, and offers on balance transfers or 0% interest may benefit you if you need to borrow money. Otherwise, they're a poor tool for earning Avios. I'd tend to avoid these cards unless you had researched the market thoroughly and decided they were a good deal for you - I wouldn't really consider the Avios in the equation.

Credit Cards: Burn and Churn

'Professional' collectors of frequent flyer miles like to 'burn and churn' credit cards. What this means is that they open a new credit card, and spend enough to trigger the initial sign up bonus. As you can see, this bonus can be as much as 20,000 Avios.

Once they've earned that, they may then cancel the credit card. Six months to years down the line, they might sign up again, rinse and repeat, earning another 20,000 (or however many!) Avios.

I'm not going to argue the pros and cons of this approach. All I will say is that you're messing with your credit record - and if you need a mortgage (or similar) in a few years, it might not be a smart move.

If you choose to go ahead, you should wait at least six months before re-applying for cards.

Less Aggressive Techniques for Quick Earning

If you're not such a fan of the burn'n'churn technique, there is a less aggressive way to earn a substantial amount of Avios quickly.

If you open one of the American Express cards, there's a section of their online banking site which allows you to 'refer a friend' to open their own card.

You'll earn a few thousand Avios for each successful referral.

Consider referring your partner and any friends who might be interested: this is a legitimate way for you to earn Avios. (They'll also get their sign-up bonus as normal).

Using Credit Card Bonus Vouchers to get More From Your Avios

The bonus vouchers offered with the Avios-earning credit cards have the potential to make your miles go much, much further.

The 'free upgrade' voucher offered by the Lloyds card can be a really nice bonus. It offers either an upgrade for one person on both legs of a BA return flight; or two one way upgrades if you're travelling as a couple.

You can only claim this voucher on bookings made via Avios.com.

Although this voucher is advertised as an 'upgrade voucher', that's not quite how it works. Essentially, you just need to look for the Avios seats you want (if you're travelling as a two, the seats must be in the same cabin). Found the two Premium Economy seats you wanted? Perfect - just click on them and choose them. You'll be charged the Avios cost for two Economy seats. If you've found the European Business class seats you wanted, bingo! Just choose them. You'll only be charged the Avios cost for two Economy (as, in Europe, planes only have Economy/Business).

Essentially, you only need Avios availability in the cabin you want to upgrade to (sit in). It doesn't matter if there's no availability in the cabin below (which you technically 'upgrade from'): you just pay the Avios cost for the cheaper cabin.

This voucher can save you quite a lot of Avios if used carefully. Note the provisos: if you upgrade to a luxurious cabin, you may need to pay a bit more in tax; and it cannot be used to upgrade from Business to First.

> When you earn this voucher, it will appear in your avios.com account. You can then apply it to any booking you'd like to make.

The voucher offered by the British Airways Amex is definitely the most desirable. You can earn one voucher per year when you hit either £10,000 of spending on the Premium card (which has the annual fee), or after £20,000 of annual spend on the free card.

As I mentioned before, if you're going to get close to £10,000 of spend, it's really worth taking out the card with the annual fee. The voucher is valuable, and you earn more Avios on day-to-day spend, too.

There's another bonus of the voucher offered with the Premium card, and that is that it has a two-year expiry date. (The voucher offered on the free card expires after a year). This makes it much more flexible - remember that, to bag the very best Avios seats, you need to book a year in advance anyway.

Effectively, the voucher is a 'buy one get one free' - when you pay for a return BA Avios reward seat, a companion comes with you (in the same plane, in the same cabin) for free. They just need to pay their own taxes and charges.

The main proviso is that there must be two reward seats available - one for you and one for them. You can only claim this voucher on bookings made via the BA Exec Club. It's also worth mentioning that only flights operated by BA can be booked with this special voucher. It doesn't count for 'codeshare' flights- for example, the intercity flights in South Africa which are flown by an airline called Comair, but with BA branding.

This voucher is a very popular deal, simply because it can make your Avios go much further than they otherwise would. Instead of having to find a whopping 240,000 Avios for an off-peak return to New York for two people in business class, you just need 120,000 Avios. So, if you're saving up for a big trip, this makes it much easier to reach your target.

Because this deal is so popular, lots of people have used different tricks and techniques to maximise its value. Here's how you can make the most of it.

Extending the validity of the BA/Amex Voucher

As I previously mentioned, the voucher given away with the Premium card has a two year validity, and the standard card has one year.

You are awarded the voucher a day or two after you hit the spending total on the Amex card. (You get a year to meet the spend total from the date the card is opened; and a max of one voucher a calendar year).

If you want to have the voucher in your pocket for as long as possible, you could stop spending at, say, £9,999 and put the card in a drawer. At the last possible moment, before your year ends, spend that last pound. The voucher validity starts from the date you cross the spend threshold.

Downgrading Your BA/Amex Voucher

This is a cunning trick. You can sign up for the Premium BA card for one year and, once you've earned your voucher (remember, the threshold is £10,000 lower to reach it!) you can call up Amex and ask them to downgrade your card to the free option. This saves you paying the repeat annual fee for the more expensive card, and it means you keep your voucher for the full two year validity (you'd lose it if you cancelled the card altogether).

Mixed Class Bookings with the BA/Amex Voucher

It's absolutely no problem to use the voucher to book an outbound leg in Business class and the return in Economy. BA.com will be able to price it up for you.

Mixed City Bookings ('open jaw') with the BA/Amex Voucher

It is possible to book an outbound flight to one city, and a return flight from another city.

As an example, it's absolutely fine to book a flight out to San Francisco, and a return from LA. The BA website will not be able to work this out for you, but the call centre will be able to.

The official rule is that any 'open jaw' route is permitted as long as the distance between the two destination airports (ie, between San Francisco and LA) is shorter than the flight distance between either airport and London. (You don't need to worry too much about this, it just means you can't get too clever and start planning round-the-world trips using the voucher).

Booking to competitive destinations with the BA/Amex Voucher

As I've previously alluded to, finding Avios availability on certain routes can be very tricky indeed.

You might need to be up at 00.00, 355 days before the flight, to grab one of the four economy (or two business) seats which are guaranteed upon the plane.

There's a problem here, of course - you'll only be able to book the outbound ticket, as the return won't yet be available.

What you need to do, in this instance, is to use the BA voucher to book the two outbounds as single tickets. When the return tickets become available, just give BA an immediate phone call and ask them to amend the booking, making it a return trip using the American Express voucher.

They usually have no problem in doing this for you, and will generally waive the £35 change fee that they usually apply to amended tickets.

Pause for a moment

Let's pause for a moment and consider a couple of existential questions. Is there really any point to any of this?

I'm enthusiastic about the value of Avios, but I'd advise you not to get too seduced by the programme.

The first point is that British Airways, and its subsidiary company which issues Avios, aren't offering any of this out of the good of their hearts. They know full well that Avios encourage customers to be loyal and to rationalise spending extra money on a BA flight, compared to a ticket with Easyjet or another airline.

They also know - very well - that it's supremely profitable to give customers a taste of flying in more expensive seats. Many people who've never flown in a Business class airline seat would never, ever consider paying the money to do so from their own pocket. However, these same people might feel more comfortable about trying the experience out if the opportunity comes up via a 'free' upgrade with Avios, or a free redemption seat.

BA know quite well that flying in a higher class than Economy is pleasurable (whereas a long haul Economy flight is anything but). Their marketing team understand that it's much easier to upsell customers with a taste of the good life into buying expensive seats in the future.

There's another thing to consider. Are Avios really ever truly free? If you were always going to buy your shopping at Tesco, perhaps they are, but don't forget that you could use them as cash and get money off your weekly shop. Is that better value than these 'free' flights?

Without delving too deep into consumer psychology, we're all irrational beings that make decisions, well, not entirely logically. For some reason, we might find ourselves spending more than we really need to, just to get our hands on a bunch of loyalty points. If you find yourself getting too far sucked in, try to check yourself: what's this really worth? And can I really afford it?

The Expert's Section

The purpose of this book isn't to delve too deeply into the overwhelming complexity of frequent flyer programmes. However, there are some advanced level tricks in earning and using Avios which I'd like to include.

This chapter is definitely only for use when you've mastered the earlier sections!

Using Iberia Plus... firstly for flights between the UK and Spain

Image by Marcos Martinez

If you're planning on redeeming Avios points to fly to Spain, or would consider beginning a long haul trip from Spain, it's worth opening up an Iberia Plus account.

I mentioned Iberia Plus early in the book, where I discussed the different possible 'accounts' for holding your Avios. At that stage, I said that this account wasn't something to worry about too much.

However, there're always exceptions to the rule... and now we're delving into the 'advanced' level Avios techniques.

As BA and Iberia are sister airlines, they've standardised the number of Avios required to fly between the UK and Spain, and so it isn't technically any cheaper to book a Spanish ticket on Iberia than it is with BA.

However.... remember the off peak/peak scheduling? Well, Iberia's peak and off-peak calendar is totally different to BA's. The upshot is that, if you're booking to Spain and the dates are 'peak' on the BA calendar, it may be worth checking what Iberia classify these dates as.

If Iberia have them as 'off peak', you're in luck - book through them and you'll save a few thousand Avios each way.

There's one little problem here - to transfer Avios across to an Iberia account, you need to have 'activated' that Iberia Plus account by earning at least one Avios in it, and then waiting for 90 days (!). It's actually not hard to earn that lone Avios - sign up for an Iberia account and look for surveys or free Avios offers on their shopping portal. Alternatively, you could transfer a small slug of points from a hotel loyalty programme to your Iberia account. It's worth jumping through this hoop today, so your Iberia Plus account is activated and ready should you need it in the future.

> One simple way to open up your Iberia Plus account is to credit Avios from a survey company - for example, eRewards - across to them. (See the 'Earning Avios' section, earlier).

...And Using Iberia Plus for Long Haul Routes

Iberia is a bit of a law unto itself and so, although BA and IB have technically standardised the number of Avios needed to travel to each destination, the reality is a little different.

As it stands, certain redemptions - most notably New York - are much cheaper in both cash and in Avios when travelling on Iberia in Business class from Madrid, and booking through Iberia.com.

On Iberia, an economy return ticket to New York comes in at 34,000 Avios off-peak, and a return Business ticket comes in at 68,000 Avios.

To compare, the BA return prices are 26,000 Avios for Economy, and 100,000 Avios for Business on off peak dates. So Iberia's Business class ticket is 32,000 Avios cheaper, and they also charge about £350 less in taxes and fees.

Of course, not everyone is going to want to fly via Madrid to New York (and, of course, you'll need to purchase the UK to Madrid flight separately, eating into your savings). However, if you're looking for a destination which both Iberia and BA fly to - generally somewhere in North or South America - it can be worthwhile to search first on the Iberia site.

On the outskirts of the zones

As we saw earlier, British Airways group destinations into nine zones, based upon distance in miles from London. Each zone has a different cost in Avios for redemption flights.

As a result, you'll encounter occasional oddities in pricing. For example, zone one contains Manchester, Milan and Munich - meaning that an Avios return ticket to the Mersey costs the same as a return to Germany.

There are many other oddities - Barcelona, for example, just falls into zone two, meaning that an Avios return to the city costs the same as a return to Dubrovnik, which is a substantially longer flight.

Of course, BA need to draw the line somewhere, and so there's not much that can be done about it. However, some enterprising souls have calculated the very best value redemptions to maximise the zone mapping.

One of the headline deals presently available is travelling from Dublin to Boston with Aer Lingus (the Irish partner of BA).

Because the flight just falls beneath the 3,000 mile boundary, it sneaks below the line into zone four. This means that an off peak Economy return is just 20,000 Avios; and Business class return just 62,500 Avios (compared to 26,000 and 100,000 Avios respectively with BA from London). The taxes are also substantially less - under £100, as opposed to more than £400 on BA.

Short haul flights on Oneworld, using Avios

Avios don't just need to be used for flights which begin or end in the UK.

In fact, some of the best value redemptions are for flights which take place in other countries, upon BA's partner airlines.

Because BA is a member of the Oneworld alliance of airlines, these opportunities are freely open to you when you have a BA Executive Club account which holds Avios. You just need to search for the flights on BA.com.

Some of BA's partner airlines include:

- American Airlines (obviously the USA, but great connections to the Caribbean, too)
- Qantas (Australasia)
- Cathay Pacific (Hong Kong, but with excellent connections to China and South East Asia)
- Finnair (Finland)
- JAL (Japan's airline)

All of these airlines offer short haul flights - either domestically or to neighbouring countries.

You'll often find excellent availability of these short haul flights, and the prices can be extremely competitive to boot. They are often much better value than taking long-haul trips.

Here are a few examples, to get you thinking:

- **American Airlines.** From New York to Chicago: 7,500 Avios each way in Economy, plus £14 in taxes and fees;

- **Quantas.** From Sydney to Melbourne: 4,500 Avios each way in Economy, plus £8 in taxes and fees;

- **Japan Airlines.** From Tokyo to Osaka: 4,500 Avios each way in Economy, plus £1.50 in taxes and fees (yes, £1.50, that's not a typo);

- **Cathay Pacific's Dragonair (a subsidiary airline).** From Hong Kong to Siem Reap, Cambodia (for Angkor Wat temples): 7,500 Avios each way in Economy, plus £10 in taxes and fees.

The Avios totals are calculated according to that same zonal map we covered earlier in the book. Rather than the zone starting in London, of course, it runs from your origin airport. Zone 1 prices apply to flights travelling 1-650 miles; Zone 2 from 651 - 1,150 miles; and so on.

As you can see, some of these deals are brilliant value for money. You'd usually be paying a couple of hundred pounds for each of the flights above - and instead you're paying a relatively small number of Avios, plus a very low amount of tax (the £1.50 within Japan is particularly impressive).

There are also OK deals to be had with Iberia's internal flights in Spain - including those across to the Canary or Balearic islands - although they're not as outstanding as any of the above.

The prices in Avios for the above flights are calculated to the banding table that you can see earlier in the book.

However, there is one small catch. There used to be exceptional deals with very short haul flights on American Airlines (internal short haul around East Coast USA). In the good old days, hopping onto one of these internal flights was a bargain, as the distances technically fell into 'zone one' and taxes were very low. However, these deals were a bit too good to be true, and BA have now upped the Avios required.

Snatching Seats on New Routes

When British Airways or Iberia launch a new route, or when they announce increased frequency of an existing route (for example, when British Airways launched a Gatwick to New York service this year), a glut of new Avios seats come onto the market.

This is because British Airways and Iberia make guaranteed numbers of redemption seats available on each plane. When a new route is launched, Avios seats suddenly become available for every single flight which will take place in the next year. So, if you're quick, you can generally take your pick of Avios seats with 'wide open' availability.

It's worth keeping an eye on British Airways or Iberia's email newsletters so you don't miss one of these opportunities.

Where Not To Use Your Avios

You're also able to redeem Avios on certain products at Avios.com. These include Eurostar tickets; hotel stays; and 'experiences' - things like packaged theatre trips to London, or luxury car racing.

Almost without exception, these represent a very poor use of your Avios.

The exchange rate for these experiences - as calculated by Avios.com - is mean, usually about 0.6p per point. In addition, these are all high margin items, where it's very easy to obtain a substantial discount (10% or more off) by looking for voucher codes somewhere on the internet, or going through a cashback retailer like Topcashback.

The reason that Avios.com is compelled to offer these things is because a lot of people struggle to find the flights they want, and, frustrated, want to redeem their Avios on something.

You now know better ;)

Don't Miss a single Avios Deal!

Thanks very much for reading this book. I hope it's given you all you need to start planning a trip of a lifetime.

Of course, Avios often launch special deals and promotions. These deals never last for long, so there's a risk that you might miss out on something fantastic!

So you don't miss out on any promotion, I've created an exclusive mailing list for people who've purchased my book - and I'll use it only to keep you up to date with the hottest Avios developments.

Simply visit www.flyupgraded.com and sign up.

I promise no spam: only the very greatest deals that you really can't miss.

I'll also send occasional tips, tricks and techniques to boost your collecting and help you discover some of the most incredible experiences, anywhere in the world.

Visit www.flyupgraded.com and sign up.

Any Further Questions?

I'm very happy to try and answer your questions about Avios. Please email questions@flyupgraded.com and I'll do my best to answer.

And finally: have you enjoyed this book?

If so, please leave a review on Amazon! Your words make a huge difference to others. Thank you.